GOTHIC RIOT DREAMS

RON GAVALIK

Pittsburgh Poet

First Edition

Published by Pittsburgh Poet
Pittsburgh, Pennsylvania
Author: Ron Gavalik
Proofreading and Editing: Rebecca Hoffman
Cover and Book Layout: Pittsburgh Poet Contributors

ISBN-13: 978-1-7320697-4-9

Experience more works by Ron Gavalik at
PittsburghPoet.com

For pap, whose unconditional love, unwavering faith, and devotion to social democracy provided me the wisdom to survive a world bent on greed and violence.

When I was a boy, in the years between preschool and first grade, my mother began to lose her mind. The rigors of being a single parent after three years of a doomed marriage brought on a form of seething rage that simmered under the surface of daily life. Dad was a far more easy-going fellow, but he preferred pool halls to home and co-workers to family. His occasional presence let loose butterflies that tickled the inside of my stomach. Unfortunately for us both, he had no intention to change the infrequency of our visits, let alone rescue me from the madness.

For these reasons and many others, my mother's parents insisted I live with them. Their logic was simple. Mom and dad wanted their freedom. Pap and gram, they wanted me.

Life with the grandparents provided early wisdom. Up until I was about ten years old, pap worked as a union boilermaker, who always left for the job early before the sun rose. During the days after school, Gram taught me how to play pinochle, gin, and rummy. "You've got to follow the cards," she said. "If you know what's been played, you've got it made." Once I learned the hustle, she had me winning quarters from rubes in bars and card parties at friends' homes in our depressed railroad town outside of Pittsburgh.

During those card games, I soaked in gram's stories about her life, raised as the unwanted black sheep by an aunt and uncle after her mother died in childbirth. I also listened intently to gram's friends, who'd also walked on the smoky side of the line. Their words and mannerisms, missing fingers and pockmarked faces, it all fascinated me from a time before I could properly write simple sentences.

On days off from school, Gram loaded me up in her station wagon for Meals on Wheels deliveries. From those early years, I witnessed firsthand the ravages of poverty and age in a forgotten America. Elderly men and women in chronic agony and barely able to speak, they sat upon broken chairs, imprisoned in roach-infested tenements. The stale air inside these joints always carried scents of dust and urine. Gram set out their trays. Sometimes she fed them while spinning gossip about local politicians.

During these visits, it was my job to never let gram's purse touch the floor.

One time, a decrypt old woman named Florence wept while gram cut and forked bits of the lady's chicken. Thick white strands of saliva formed in the corners of Florence's mouth as she chewed. The woman scratched her arms with curled hands plagued with arthritis. Her skin reminded me of an almost transparent tracing paper from school drawing projects. Trying not to stare, I shifted my focus to the ancient red rug that covered the floor's planks. The fabric, weakened by time, crumbled when I stubbed it with my sneakers.

"Keep chewing," gram said. "You're doing well."

"I love you, Dolly," Florence said between bites. "I would die without you."

Completely unable to accept a compliment, Gram refused to smile. She simply said, "Better you die than me."

Florence laughed so hard I could smell her diarrhea breath across the room. I thought that woman would keel over right there. Instead, she farted and then waved her claw at me.

Gram and I headed back to the house in the late afternoons so she could start cooking dinner.

In the evenings, pap stumbled through the back door into the kitchen, his clothes and face covered in soot, his body exhausted. Sometimes I'd run up to him and hug his leg in a sign of a child's unfiltered love. Pap always laughed in delight, and then he'd pat my back in approval.

As I clung to those dirty work pants, the sharp smell of burnt metal filled my world. That scent hung in the air around the steel mills and railyards, a reflection of the gritty region, its culture of hard day labor and heavy Sunday dinners.

In short, this was our definition of the good life.

At the beginning of my adult life, I regularly stopped by the house for visits and to cut the grass, rake leaves, or shovel snow. As a young father and wannabe writer, I required regular doses of wisdom from the people who loved me the most.

Confined to a hospital bed in the living room, gram drifted in and out of consciousness. After a kiss hello, I'd listen to the dying woman tell me she was going to "get better" and someday "go back to Florida." Gram adored the sun and the sand almost as much as she revered the power of denial.

On several occasions, I asked her if she'd bring me back a souvenir. Her answers were always the same. "No. You and your mother think we're made of money."

In the summer, Pap and I often sat together on the back porch glider, surrounded by his stacks of novels, history books, healthy eating cookbooks, and his worn copy of the Catechism of the Catholic Church. Our discussions epitomized blue collar philosophy, simple words to express complex views. Pap loved debating the virtues of unions and socialism vs. the evils of corporate capitalism.

On one summer Saturday, pap's tabletop hibachi filled the air with the scent of barbecue. After enduring triple bypass heart surgery fifteen years earlier, the old man had given up grease, caffeine, sugar, and fun. Instead, he relished in learning new heart-friendly recipes. His food tasted like bland sadness, but as is true with most things in our lives, circumstance drives desire.

"How come you never wanted to go anywhere?" I said.

"What do you mean? I go places."

"I don't mean the grocery store. You and gram barely traveled. There's a whole world out there."

"I saw it all during the war," he said. Pap had served as a ball turret gunner in a bomber during World War II. "Trees in Italy look no different than trees in Pittsburgh."

"You're such a curmudgeon."

Pap chuckled while flipping his chicken breast. "You can't rush chicken. You've got to let the medicine cook deep."

Pap's so-called *medicine* was code for some flu-staving concoction he read about in a magazine. The brownish liquid he'd thrown together resembled a jar of vomit: Scotch whiskey and a mystery fluid, mixed with diced herbs and vegetables.

"I think it's delicious," he said.

Pap put the lid back on the hibachi and spread out on the glider. The barbecue smoke that encompassed us triggered my memory of the long-gone metallic odor once embedded in his work clothes. I hadn't noticed its absence until that day.

"I miss that smell."

Pap kind of frowned and rolled his eyes in that way when we hear the young and naïve speak without experience. "I don't." He then pointed his spatula at me. "What's that shirt you're wearing?"

"Metallica, why?" I'd worn an old *...And Justice for All* concert t-shirt to cut his lawn.

"That music is too violent for me."

"More violent than labor riots in the thirties? How about civil rights in the sixties?"

Pap's eyes widened behind his glasses and he sat up straight. "Those movements were for the working man. People with nothing were gunned down for trying to make an honest living and be left in peace."

"Yes, pap, I know."

"Out there in the freezing cold, strikers in Homestead refused to leave the line until Frick and Carnegie murdered them. Then down in the south, the bigots went after those sanitation workers. They beat the blacks to death or hung them from trees. The workers still wouldn't stop until they got some dignity. It really was a sight to see."

A little tweak at the old man to defend my choice of music had turned into a labor protest. Whenever we discussed the pursuit of democracy, blood-soaked images ran through my mind of fathers and sons, women and the elderly, clubbed half to death by those whose supremacy was threatened.

"That struggle was a gothic existence," I said.

"How is it gothic?"

"There's a gloom that surrounds people who never know if they're going to make it. The struggle to survive without any rights to a home or food is gothic. It's similar to what serfs dealt with in Europe during the dark ages."

Pap looked out into the small yard where his tomato plants grew. "You know, those right-wingers on the radio, they got people fooled. Everyone hates unions now. I don't know what young guys like you are going to do."

"The only thing we can do, I suppose, work and pray."

"Yes," pap said, his focus still on the tomato plants. "Work and pray. That's right." After a moment of his pondering, the old man chuckled. "You're a writer now, aren't you?"

"I'm working on it."

"Maybe someday when your grandmother and I are gone, you'll write a book about how people still have to put up with this horse shit."

Twenty years later, that's exactly what I did.

Acknowledgements

There's a hidden beauty amongst those of us who must work every day, paycheck to paycheck, just to feed ourselves and pay the bills. During breaks at the jobs, we breathe. When we should be sleeping, we imagine. The lovers we choose and the children we raise, they embody beautiful risks to our bank accounts and to our health. In this free verse poetry collection, I've captured some of those moments of fear and regret, joy and sadness, that exist within each of us.

There are propagandized fools among us who believe shining a light of truth on our gothic lives is tantamount to rebellion. Terms such as *solidarity* and *democracy* are regarded as a subversive evil that must be stricken from our vocabularies. Such hatred reminds me of the moral leaders who suffered violence, all so we could have a better future.

With that said, I am humbly grateful to those who've made Gothic Riot Dreams possible. As I've noted in other books, Rebecca Hoffman is my editor and most trusted literary ally. Her careful attention to detail is the stuff of dreams. I am also thankful and indebted to my TRUE Readers, the amazing patrons who've invested in my ongoing literary pursuits.

Among my TRUE Readers, there are two champions who've devoted the necessary funding to publish this collection. I give special thanks and my unending adoration to **Holly Kudyba** and **Rebecca Shortman**. Both of these beautiful souls know what it is to fight and love and thrive in a treacherous world. Their strength is an example for us all.

It's now time to begin. No matter our cultural or individual differences, in these pages we are all brothers and sisters. That invisible connection extends beyond friendship. Bonded by our mutual struggle to make it, we are indeed family.

—Ron Gavalik

"While there is a lower class, I am in it, while there is a criminal element, I am of it, and while there is a soul in prison, I am not free."

—Eugene V. Debs

THE WORK WHISTLE BLOWS

Hard Labor Love

I came up in Pittsburgh,
the Rust Belt of hard labor
with a deep love of community.
As children, we collected railroad spikes
from the tracks and we cut our shins
on random iron shards in slag hills.
Some of us were union middle-class
while others breathed the gray air of poverty.
That hardly mattered.
As we stood atop foothills
that overlooked the city skyline,
soot embedded under our fingernails,
we lived as kings and queens
who oversaw the future.

Embrace TRUTH

The cost of TRUTH
may at times burden
our mental energy and our wallets,
especially when we are delivered
so many cheap, comfortable lies.
TRUTH, however, is the tonic
that heals and fortifies our minds
against the constant flood of toxic oil
that pours from the gullets
of poseurs and profiteers.

The few who summon the courage
to embrace TRUTH are transformed
into angels of light. They rise above
the sewage of violence and hatred
of so many polluted minds.
These angels then fly over
the diseased souls,
those condemned
to wither in misery.

Age of Innocence

As a child in elementary school,
we learned the basic horrors
of slavery and war.
In one history class,
I endeavored to understand
how men and women could exploit
other humans to the point of collapse.
The sickness of greed,
it seemed so obvious that any fool
could recognize its malicious symptoms.
When I grew up and worked
my first minimum wage job,
memories from that class
had resurfaced, and finally,
I began to understand.

Obdurate

On a construction site
as the sun rose over the hill,
I watched as my fellow applicants
humbly and quietly lined up
for unskilled labor jobs.
Those men, I figured,
they have fat wives
and beautiful marriages.
I couldn't bring myself
to stand behind them,
and so I walked off.

Sitting in the bar,
a few raindrops fell
onto the stained glass window
above the top shelf liquor,
just out of reach. An old drunkard
stared me down with the crook eye.
'Young guy like you should work.
What are you doing here?'
I didn't respond.
There was nothing to say,
besides, drink always goes down
a little smoother when guilt
eats us from within.

Found Will

A tear fell
onto Eve's cheekbone.
It clung to her flesh.
The sadness inside,
she tried to cast it away,
but the sadness held on.
It refused to drip onto the floor.
Eventually, Eve grabbed a tissue,
and with determination,
she wiped the sadness
from her life.

Cockroaches

On a bitter cold fall day, a neighbor
knocked on the door.
He asked for a can of roach spray
and a drinking glass.
He had a plan to escape
all the cockroaches
and their demands.

In the distance, a countless number
of brown leaves fell away
from the trees on the hillside.
They'd given up and slowly
floated to their demise.

I handed the neighbor a glass
and poured a heavy shot of bourbon.
The man then wept
as a prisoner whose parole
had finally come.

Liberated

The day I walked off a job
without having another lined up,
the most pronounced emotion
that bubbled up through the noise
in my mind was the scream of liberation.
Positive as that may be,
most people equate self-determination
with the tranquility of happiness.
Certainly, one can lead to the other,
but that's not the usual.
Staring at the stack of bills
shows us the treacherous bridge
that we must build to span the divide
between freedom
and the ability to live.
That bridge requires
our sweat and torment,
our blood and our tears,
and often times,
our souls.

Drama Free

The crazy old woman
in the ratty red sweater
who sits on a bench outside
the bookstore,
she waves to everyone
who passes by.
She thinks everyone is a long lost friend.
Most people ignore the woman,
but they should pay attention.
She's got the game
all figured out.

Con Game

Speaking false words
you believe others want to hear
while withholding truth,
so you can persuade people
to your beliefs,
that's the oldest con game.

Sure, you may win
in the short-term,
but people eventually catch on.
In the end, the con
is a great way to lose
the argument, the battle,
your miserable life.

Rotten Tip

A good piece of fish,
that brand new job smell
that fills the air with possibilities,
and houseguests:
they all go bad
after three days.

Down and Gone

Back in my bartending days,
I worked at a shitty motel.
They needed a big man
to scare off the hustlers and whores.
There was this one woman that came in
several nights a week. She was middle-aged,
heavier in the stomach, but she still had it
in the ass and in her tortured eyes.
She always sat alone
and drank ice cold vodka doubles
like she meant business.

One time I asked her,
'What is it, baby? What are you
trying to forget?'

The dame didn't even look up at me.
Instead, she silently played with her glass.
A minute later she downed what was left,
and then strolled out of the joint.
She didn't return the next night
or the night thereafter.
I got canned a week later,
but I highly doubt
she ever went back.

Want

I often wonder
what the world wants
or expects of me.
Then I realize the truth.
All people from all places,
they search all their lives
for happiness.
Some people, their lives sucked
away by jobs, commutes, spouses,
they want and expect
me to deliver happiness
upon them.
The smart ones,
they pursue happiness
on their own terms.

My Blood

When a drop of blood
falls onto the page
of a poet's notebook
and rolls into the spine,
the blood becomes a permanent
part of each poem.
The blood is then absorbed
by every reader
for all time.

Better World

In the corner of the coffee shop,
a young illustrator works
on his drawing pad,
quiet and alone.
Around him, two girls in shorts,
tanned cleavage on display,
their painted lips suck on iced coffees,
as they await fulfillment.

The artist continues to draw,
his total focus on the visual story
is the envy of inferior men.
He’s constructing a better world,
one made up of dreams
only he can see.

My Chair

A young writer
sat in my regular chair
inside the bookstore cafe.
He banged at the keys of his typer,
angry and without mercy.
Once he drained his coffee cup
the writer kept sucking at the rim
for a few remaining drops.
He then stared blankly
at the wall for several minutes.

Defeated, the writer packed up
his supplies into a ratty backpack,
and then stomped out of the joint.
I figured my chair had enough
of the games. It felt my presence
nearby and thus decided
we had sins to paint.

Puddles

Tears of fathers and angels
fall as raindrops onto the streets.
Those drops form puddles
of red blood
that swirl with gold streaks
of remaining hope
in pavement divots
and in potholes.

Forced to endure unjust death,
these men of tormented love
awaken to the truth of sorrow.
Their minds and their bodies
and their spirits
are furious and engaged.
For the first time
in a long time,
these men are alive.

Keep Dancing

At the gas station,
two teenage girls got groovy
inside a silver sedan
while the mother pumped fuel.
'You better calm yourselves in there,'
the mom said as a warning.
'People will think you're loony.'
The girls laughed,
but they kept dancing
in their seats without shame.
Mom then began to bob her head,
and for a small moment,
it seemed she'd forgotten
the price of gas.

Food or Truth

In the grocery store,
a woman screamed at a young cashier
about the way her groceries were bagged.
The young woman behind the register,
she kept her mouth shut.
Her face twisted as her self-esteem absorbed
the sadistic punishment.
When the customer left the store,
I said to the cashier,
'You need to speak your truth.'
The girl frowned and stared down
at her keyboard, the anchor of her reality.
'I can't,' she said, almost whispering.
'My son needs to eat.'

Our Relationship

My relationship with you
resembled the way society
treats its great artists.
I loathed you in life
and celebrate you in death.
I can think of no higher praise
grounded in truth.

Moment of Freedom

The day after we lose a job,
and the shock has passed,
the mind wanders the cosmos,
easier and without interruption.
Everything feels distant,
separated, out of reach.
We are untouchable.
That brief sensation of liberation,
before the bills are due,
is the purest moment of freedom
many of us will ever live.

Hold the Line

When one pursues petty disagreements
with a brother or sister at the job,
it's sometimes easy to forget
the deep connection and the power
that lives inside the comrades
who share our struggle.
Hours, months, or years later,
when the shit hits the fan,
we may require the help
of these magnificent souls.
The strength of solidarity
reminds us we are not alone
and we never have to be
ever again.

Self-Determination

The best people
do not sit quietly
in cardboard boxes
of preconceived notions,
definitions, expectations.
The best people carry box cutters
and the know-how to wield
that tool in the struggle
to free themselves
from such prisons.

To the curb...

If a man claims
more friends than fingers,
he's either lying
to your face
or he's a fool.
I highly doubt
you need me to tell you
the next step
in the procedure.

Countdown

Sometimes we're reminded
in the great cosmic timeline
our lives begin and end
in a flap
of a hummingbird's wing.
Whatever you plan to accomplish,
you better make it happen
soon.
The meter is running,
my friend,
and it can never
be turned back.

Defiled Aura

Two women in business suits
sat at my regular table
inside the bookstore café.
I took the table next to them
so I could easily jump back
to my rightful place
after they finished their drinks.
The suits spoke as strangers
and discussed 'proactive challenges.'
When the women left the joint,
I hesitated to retake my table.
It appeared tainted,
polluted by buzzwords
and a stale odor
of conformity.

Brief Awakening

In the news, I read about a taxi driver
in New York who shot himself in the head.
The guy, in his sixties, he did the deed
on the steps in front of City Hall.
The suicide note he'd written on social media
told anyone who cared enough to know
that he was tired,
he was fucking exhausted
from working 120 hours a week
to put bread on the table.
In that man's final moments of truth,
he called himself a slave.

Most of us are slaves to the jobs,
the propaganda on TV, the internet,
and to the hyped products we buy
and never need.

Unfortunately, most of us don't realize it.
At least that taxi driver gave himself
the gift of a brief awakening
before his eternal rest.

Pride in Ruins

Hope is the realistic wish of dreamers
to build better times tomorrow
that contrast yesterday's struggles.
Miserable men and women
who blame society's ills on everyone
except themselves, they believe
hope is meaningless.

When hucksters and con-artists
use hope as the distraction
to pick the dreamers' pockets,
the miserable cheer and they howl
in self-righteous victory.

As the miserable then begin to suffer,
they blame the dreamers for hoping,
and never their own obstruction.
The miserable cannot help
the dreamers defeat con-artists
because they believe deep in their core
it's better to watch the world
burn and crumble around them.
After all, pride is far more valuable
in ruins than the work
to build better times.

Occasional Spice

Around the world,
there are uncorrupted souls
and there are miscreants of evil
we read about and see in the media.
Most of us, however, we live
neither directly in the sun
nor under the blanket of night.
We walk upon sidewalks
on partly cloudy days.
Sometimes our actions or our words
ride along the edge of dusk
to provide an occasional spice,
a reminder that no one is perfect.
Funny how so many of us
often forget
that truth.

Robbed Love

I wanted to love you,
but the jobs owned us.
Your masters scheduled you
for the evenings and late nights.
I served the desires of others
in the mornings and afternoons.

The children who will never come,
their beautiful faces have visited
me in dreams and in visions.
The boy would have enjoyed
painting in watercolors.
Our daughter could have
saved lives.

In one dream, the two of us sat
on a porch glider during retirement.
My hip ached, but it was a good day
because you held my hand
and we laughed
about an inside joke
we'll never know.

The dreams don't visit me
these days. My mind repressed
the sadness, probably so I can function
at the job, and generate profits
as I've been instructed.

The Dawn

Inside the dark box
of wage servitude,
we are drugged
by propaganda.
That's how they keep us
docile and in line.
Sometimes a servant
refuses to swallow
his prescribed meds.
In the short time
before he is silenced,
that servant's spoken truth
is acid that burns jagged holes
through the gray walls
to reveal a glimpse of sunlight.
These moments of power
are care packages
for the mind and the soul
that never erode
or fade away.

Let Go

When we work a job,
there's a true sense of investment
in the company, the tasks,
the shared experiences with others.
Then the boss reminds us,
with the forked tongue of a caustic lover,
that our minds and our bodies
are quite simply disposable.
In such desperate times,
we question our self-worth
and spend our evenings wondering
just what went wrong.

Exhausted from analysis,
our minds finally let go.
We fly away from the prison
in hope, and we ponder
the possibility of better times
that may lie ahead.

Duplicitous

Wherever human life exists,
there are those who pay homage
to the ravenous, the aggressive.
Gutless cowards, afraid
of their own shadows,
they enjoy handing over power
to the hustlers and whores
who reign supreme.

In these societies,
the kind and the gentle
don't stand a chance.
We often pretend
fealty for lambs
while we stand in line
to glorify the tyranny
of lions.

Use the Sadness

There's a sadness
that flows through the veins
of people who survive empire.
For some, the sadness transforms
into a base fear of the unknown,
cowardice validated by con-artists
in the open air, and by charlatans
who profit deep in the shadows.
The sadness in others can transform
into courage, a rage fueled by the thirst
for truth and moral balance.
Sadness that leads to action
to correct injustices,
that's the only possible deliverance
from anguish and despair.

Holy Place

There's a small space
between the tip of a pen
and the fibers of notebook paper.
As it is with many truths,
that space cannot be seen.
Still, that tiny chasm is a universe
upon itself, a holy place
where the miracle
of one's soul is labored,
bled out, streamed
into the physical world
for others to read
and feel and know.

Stand Tall

There is no justice
or education or community
behind the walls of backlit screens.
There is no freedom
or liberty or rights
in the shadows.
After the beat down
from the greased fists
of wealthier owners,
we've earned a long rest.
When the determination returns,
it's time to stand tall
under the sun, for all to see,
and we must walk together
in solidarity.

Personal

The bosses always tell us
their decisions are not personal.
When they hold the pay raises
we need for gas and shoes,
that cash stolen from our families
becomes quite personal.

When we have to wait
a two-week eternity
to pay the past due electric bill,
or when we pretend canned pasta
tastes like chicken with sauce,
that's fucking personal.

When the knife or the gun
feels like tangible justice in our hands,
a cool sense of control,
that's personal too.

Detect Truth

There's very little truth
to be found in people
who have much to lose.
On the other hand,
there's an abundance of truth
that pours out of the mouths
of children, cancer patients,
scorned lovers,
and our recently fired
brothers and sisters
at the job.

The Eternal Fight

Imagine you've been tortured,
ridiculed, hated by the masses.
As you bleed to death on top of a hill
for suggesting people give a damn,
another tortured soul asks you
to forgive his sins.
The man did nothing to you,
but he feels the need to confess.
Writhing in pain, you want to die,
if only to end your own torment.
But instead, you listen to the man,
and you grant him his desire,
which is your truest sense of love.
You tell the bloodied dissident
he will soon be in paradise,
and you fucking mean it.

That's why some of us cannot reconcile
ourselves to the corporate structure.
We are only satisfied in the fight
for our brothers and sisters,
the marginalized, the despised.
The bosses and their political front men
can kill us, as they so often do,
but in our struggle, we know
they will never win.

Read in Peace

There's something liberating
about watching old men
with gray beards and hats
read intently from thick books
while the world unfolds around them.
Their families are gone,
along with the desire to chase
fast women and fast cash.

These aged men of leisure,
they are the survivors
of war and capitalism,
religion and disease.

Nothing surprises these old men
in their final days of wisdom,
and so, it’s quite simple.
They read in peace.

LUNCH BREAK WHISTLE

Funeral Procession

Standing on the corner, waiting to cross the street
during a lunch break at the job,
a long funeral procession drove through the intersection.
The hearse and the limousine appeared washed,
they shined under the winter sun.
The other cars were older,
filthy from salt and road dirt.

No one had time for car washes
when their friend or relative
lay dead in a box.

Most of the cars in the endless line
were driven by young men, jaws clenched,
their eyes focused straight on the road ahead.
In some of the passenger seats, young women
sat quiet, their eyes puffy and red
as their attention roamed the city.

Eventually the cars stopped at a red light.
One sedan was stuck in the middle of the intersection,
driven by an older man, alone.
His eyes met mine, but he stared through me.
I removed my hat and bowed my head,
a gesture in a world we can't understand
or hope to control.

The procession began to move forward.
Before the man drove off,
he formed a slight smile

under his tortured eyes.
In those few seconds,
he and I mourned together as brothers,
without names or histories.
It didn't really matter
that we were strangers.

Gothic Riot Dreams

Looking out over the east end of Pittsburgh
atop the roof of a parking garage,
faint cries from a small band
of poverty-stricken residents
could be heard in the distance.

In the face of violent greed,
tormented souls spewed anger.
Many howled pleas for mercy.
Others begged on their knees
to keep their homes
in the only community
they've ever known.

The commoners' impassioned prayers,
unabsorbed by the suits who peered down
from their luxury balconies,
floated upwards into the sky
to form an expansive white cloud.

After a while, the crowd's energy waned,
their words could no longer feed the cloud.
A strong wind then came through.
The people, helpless to its power,
watched as the current carried away
our gothic riot dreams.

Fog

Over years of sin,
the memories, the faces,
they're obscured by a fog
of whiskey and regret.
But I never really hurt anyone.
I was far too busy
damaging myself.

Cookie Conquest

In the bookstore café,
at a table near the window,
a father and his young boy
ate oversized cookies.
A shopping bag lay on the floor
under the table. The bag contained
a colorful graphic novel of some kind
and a dense history book.
The smiles on their faces
revealed pride, as if they celebrated
a successful hunt, a true conquest.
Once those men finished consuming
their sweet rewards, the father carried
the empty plates back to the counter.
He then took his boy by the hand
and they walked out
into the spring sun
as champions.

Skinny Cigarettes

The old cashier at the car dealership,
she chain-smoked skinny, long cigarettes
all day, every day.
Her voice sounded like a bullfrog
that recently learned how to curse and laugh.
The crease lines around her mouth
and the folds in her neck
conveyed a relaxed style, confidence
earned from a hard life
and dangerous choices.

Sometimes there were no customers
in front of the cashier's window
and no mechanics around to bust her chops.
That's when she'd rest her elbows on the counter
and cradle a skinny cigarette
between two fingers near her cheek.
That woman's eyes would gaze outside,
glossed over in what looked like daydreams
about all those lovers in their graves,
and their cliché widows
with their tiresome grandchildren
and their lovely lives.

Back in the day,
men in gray suits and skinny ties
never could resist her,
but then again,
so few ever tried.

The Immortals

The way a person walks
tells the story of who they are,
who they claim to be,
and where they've been.

Rarely, but every so often,
someone will walk by
as if they're fulfilling a destiny.
These people are not necessarily in a rush
or seriously determined.
They simply swagger as immortals,
in a manner only those who've died
many times can pull off.

The immortals know their purpose,
which allows them to focus
on completing their life's work.
Everything else, the distractions
and the lovers, nonsense careers,
and tedious families,
are simply less important.

For a few seconds, while witnessing
an immortal pass on the sidewalk,
we can see they are the victors of life,
elusive heroes we may never meet
or really understand.

Four-Leaf Clover

In a Pittsburgh bookstore,
a blonde woman in jean shorts
cut up to her crotch, exposing the pocket linings
and her ass cheeks, emerged from the book stacks.
She casually strolled into the café
and pitched a coffee cup in the trashcan.
A tattoo of a four-leaf clover
adorned the inside of her upper right thigh.
The tattoo could only be seen mid-stride,
a visual gift to every patient man she passed.

About thirty-five years old,
some people might have criticized
the woman for her fashion preferences
or her life choices. Of course, the snobs
and the conservatives have their parts to play
in the world. They are the miserable darkness
that contrasts the greater light of small pleasures.

That woman clearly knew herself.
She walked with style, an earned confidence
seen in others who've survived long wars of failed jobs,
dead family members, and poor lovers.

As the woman returned to the stacks
and disappeared into the words of mad authors,
the tattoo no longer signified an indiscretion.
Her clover was a medal of survival,
a reminder that good luck comes to those
who walk through the fire with courage
and the strength to never look back.

Smeared

I don't really understand you,
your words, your actions.
Most people accept ignorance
from others
because they barely understand
themselves.

I've taken the time
and I've spent the energy
to know myself, my truth.

Your presence is a blur,
a smeared existence.
When I look at you,
my eyes feel unclean,
as if they've been dipped
in a sticky honey
that I will never be able
to wash away.

Betrayed

Watching friends and family
swallow the rich temptations
of hatred, a deep thirst for death,
that is the ultimate betrayal.
To watch on as loved ones devalue life
murders the trust and companionship
that took a lifetime to build.
Alone and heartbroken,
betrayed,
we are left to wander aimless
into the gravity well
of madness.

One Buck

A homeless man near an on-ramp
of the parkway in Pittsburgh
held a sign that read,
'I just want to see you smile.'
A man in a car with his woman
pulled over to the curb.
The woman rolled down her window
and handed the bum a buck.
After a quick chat, the couple waved
to the homeless man, and then drove off.

People say a dollar buys nothing
in this day and age.
Those three people
may disagree.

Overcome

At a local park, a little boy of about five
tried over and over again to scale
a child-sized rock climbing wall.
Over and over again, he'd lose his grip
and fall into the grass
while his father watched.

A little girl of about the same age
swung on the swing set while her mother
pushed and smiled.

Eventually, the woman said to the man,
'Why don't you help him?'
The man chuckled.
'I'm waiting for the girl
to pitch in.'

On the boy's 432nd failed attempt,
the little girl ran over to the wall
and pushed on the boy's butt
until he swung his leg over
the top of the wall.
Both of the children cheered
at their achievement.

'Now they know teamwork,'
the mother said.
The father nodded.
'They learned solidarity.'

Skimmed

A flock of ducks on the riverbank
wobbled through the grass, scrounging
for bugs and crumbs with their silly duck bills.
The birds mindlessly walked around
following each other, quacking and nibbling
the way ducks do.

There was one colorful mallard,
he didn't seem concerned with the flock.
His truth led him away
to find dinner elsewhere.

A few of the other ducks quacked at him
for flaunting his responsibility
to do what was expected.

That colorful duck ignored them all,
as if their opinions meant nothing.
He did his own scrounging in style
while the sun skimmed the skyscrapers
before it set for the evening.

Tossed

An empty wine bottle
covered in grime
lay on its side in the gravel
parking lot of a local flea market.
For a short time, someone coveted
that bottle as a small treasure.
It represented a break
from a shit life or a shit job.
Once the last drop was consumed,
that bottle was tossed aside,
much like the memories
that live within the trinkets
for sale at the vendor tables.

Devotion

When brutality on the streets
becomes so daunting,
and the struggle for peace
overwhelms our senses,
that exhaustion leads to
the desire to lie down
and give in to hate.

Take heart in the exhaustion.
It's a healthy part of love.
After a good rest,
a devoted spirit is then ready
to carry on the struggle
for justice.

Euphony

When the music is absent at the job
or on the bus, we often swim
in thoughts of darkness.
Powerful memories once repressed,
they resurface to streak their oil
through the mind.

In these times, we forget
the tranquility rhythm can bring.
After a while, we stumble upon the music again.
It reminds us that we are spiritual beings
of passion and purpose.

Music, much like air, fills gaps
throughout our lonely days
and strengthens our bonds with others.
Music sweeps us into flight
above the trees and petty hatred,
away from the pollution
of broken hearts and soiled spirits.
In music, we are strong
because we are whole.
We are forever.

Ant's Life

A lone black ant scurried
across the tile floor in the coffee shop.
Far from its colony, the ant marched
courageously on its journey
to find food and water for others.
Halfway across the barren floor,
the ant stopped. It turned to look
back at the road traveled, and then
turned to view the road to come.
The ant appeared lost
in thought or prayer.

After careful consideration,
that black ant continued its trek
across the desert landscape.
It would either fulfill its task
or risk death in the glorious attempt.
Fear, ever present, would not
control the ant's short life
or be allowed to corrupt
its moral truth.

Ron Gavalik

Nausea Daddy

Inside a swank bar
in the city, a young woman
with delicious legs and pouty lips
loudly demanded
an apple martini.

Her middle-aged benefactor,
a guy with groomed facial scruff
and wearing a designer jacket,
rolled his eyes. A smile
then formed across his face
as the girl patted his ass.

In silence, the bartender
mixed the drink.

'She just sucked me off,'
the suit said out of nowhere.
The bartender set down the martini
and then walked away.

Pursuing Trendy

It's funny how every town and city
from New York to Pittsburgh to Portland
has embraced expensive microbreweries
and specialty whiskey bars.

These establishments serve
the yuppies and hipsters,
the corporatized young
who've discovered a fad in self-abuse.
Among like-minded friends,
beards have replaced cocks,
and money fills the void
where moral truth never
quite took hold.

The fashionable, the disloyal,
they seek a smooth intoxication
in the warmth of safe spaces,
the very features denied
to those who labor for little
and drink to forget much.

Fiendish

Sometimes I smile at random people
because I get off on watching others
smile back out of a sense of duty or obligation.
Then I read about American fascists
who rip away children
from weeping mothers, fathers,
and aging grandparents,
desperate souls on the run
from violent gangs.
That's when I frown at passersby
because that style of misery
we're forced to endure
is a necessary component
to all sadistic relationships.

Pause and Look Down

The best sidewalks
are discolored
from the blood of youth
and the tears of victims.
Those sidewalks
tell stories, they provide lessons
of hard choices under
difficult circumstances.
Jagged cracks in the concrete
resemble the struggle
of so many souls
long gone.

Judge the Judges

The innocent who pass judgement
on others for committing
rather common sins
lack the courage to truly live.
In pursuit of purity,
the pristine regularly trash
the gift of imagination,
even when it's obvious
that abandonment of adventure
is the greatest sin.

Confrontations

A man confronts adversaries
every day of his life.
At the job, he takes on his boss
and the problems of coworkers.
At the bar, a man must earn his place
among the drunkards atop their stools.
In the bedroom, he must prove himself
worthy of the woman
who spreads her thighs.
On remote trails in the woods,
a man must confront himself
and engage in spiritual combat
with his demons.

Of all the many confrontations
throughout a man's days,
only the battles with himself
lead to any lasting peace.
After a years-long struggle
to punish his lost youth,
he will finally accept his sins.

That's when a man may then truly enjoy
the rustle of trees in the breeze
and the rushing water of a stream
after the rain.

Poet's ~~Wisdom~~

Calling out dead poets
as sexists or rapists or users
is the opposite of woke enlightenment.
The poet's job is to share
his experiences or his madness,
and never self-censor his words
for sanitized comforts.

The poet's truth is his gift
of insight, a naked wisdom
of hard love and difficult choices.
Narrow fools so often absorb
this sweat and blood
poured onto the page.
After their souls are satisfied,
that's when the fools unsheathe
the long sword of ignorance
and thrust the blade square
in the poet's back.

Backlit Voracity

Nothing feels so empty
as easy satisfaction
that requires little
effort or sacrifice.
As filthy johns
in search
of the cheapest whores,
we salivate over
and consume
the spilled blood
of artists
who offer beauty
in the hopes
of small rewards.

In a gluttonous feast,
we take what we want
without apologies
and never offer
one cup of coffee
or a slice of bread.

Swindled

If corporate and political racketeers
have taught us anything, it's that
we should never underestimate
the power of sweet words
from the mouths of thieves.

No matter how deep they rape us
of our rights and our resources,
their soothing voices
make us eternally grateful
for the violence
that conquers
our lives.

Cat Conclusions

A fat orange cat lay stretched
in the grass of a city park.
The cat watched carefully
as chirping birds flew by
and bugs buzzed in the air.

An old lady in white pants
and black flip-flops
said to her husband,
'Mr. Cat over there sure has the life.'
The man in baby blue pants
and brown sandals,
he nodded his agreement.

Maybe the old lady was right,
but we'd never really know.
Each of us have our jobs,
our troubles, our stories,
and Mr. Cat has his.

To Grieve

In mourning lost friends,
our vision is tinted.
The bosses, co-workers,
and even the friends around us
become trees in distant landscapes
that sway a little slower
in the breeze.

In these moments of sorrow,
we are dark pupils that open wide
to absorb any available light
from our communities.
That devotion sometimes
fills the void where a loved one's
body once resided
and their true spirit
will forever live.

Daily Escape

Some of us drink in the bar
to escape the rain,
others to escape the sun.
Everyone has their reasons
to get away from the grind,
but not one of us has a plan
to survive it.

Puzzled

It's fascinating how people are aware
corn syrup and other chemicals
have replaced the basic ingredients
in our foods and drinks.
It is fucking puzzling how people
refuse to understand
how the unbridled power
of double-speak and propaganda
have replaced the ingredients
of our truths.

Tanned

What if we burned down
the tanning salons
and danced
around the flames?
From the ashes,
in rebirth,
we could build
union halls, art galleries,
libraries, homeless shelters.

Perhaps productive spaces
would make people
smile a little more often
in a landscape of smirks and scowls.
Of course, happiness
is not part of the business plan.
As pap would say, 'Having $10
more than the other guy makes you
feel like you got one up on him.'
Therefore, watching children starve
to death or be bombed to death
has made us feel exceptional,
content with fitness centers
and tanning beds.

Murdered Spirit

There was once a teenage poet,
a young thinker, an honors student,
a free and generous spirit.
He made those around him
feel a little better
about their poverty-stricken
and despised lives.

When the cold hand of authority
gunned down his body
in a rage of violent lust,
it was his spirit that paid the penalty
for daring to breathe free.

As the young poet's community
mourned and celebrated
their fallen son's short life,
I could not claim any such privilege.
That boy was a fellow writer,
and so, those of us who share
that passion, we mourned
in quiet for the words
that will never come.

Fabricate Consent

The tragedy of mainstream
American culture is our isolation
from reality. All societies use myths
to shape an understanding of the world,
a reason for the mysteries of the cosmos.
The myths of history were based on experiences,
scientific principles, or deep philosophies.
American myths are based almost solely
on narratives fed through electronics,
streamed directly into our minds.
Stuck in endless feedback loops
of dangerous misconceptions,
we are marionettes, robbed
of the ability to think
for ourselves.

Simpleminded

Life is so much easier
when we are told who to hate,
when to hate, and how to hate.
Men and women in suits,
they program us to consume
gluttonous messages of patriotism
made possible by generous sponsors.

As a reward for our devotion
to the party, the brand,
we are granted a delectable
two-minute hit of rage.
That orgy of sarcastic quips
and voiced violence
is the tempest
that ignites our minds
in a firestorm of emotion
that never quite reaches
a climax.

Unsatisfied, the cycle repeats.

Daydreamers

The clerk behind the coffee counter,
she stares out the window
onto the sunny street, lost in thought.
Her half smile on that young face
is an art exhibit of a daydream
about a possible future.

An old woman at a nearby table,
she stares out the same window.
Her eyes glossed over,
they indicate she's remembering
the good moments long past.

The coffee shop daydreamers
have much in common.

The Gift

There are people of substance
who explore the world around them.
They read books on buses,
help their neighbors in the evenings,
and eat delicious food with family.
These people laugh hard from the gut.
In times of sorrow, they weep
for lost friends and lost causes.
During moments of injustice,
they stand up and fight back.

Sometimes we feel surrounded
by so many unfortunate souls
who live in the perpetual fire of misery,
but when we engage in a conversation
with someone who truly lives,
we're reminded they are
a rare gift of life.

Rejuvenation

I've always enjoyed
dropping loose change
into hats of sidewalk artists.
A little recognition of those
who spill their blood
gives them reason
to keep performing
in a society
that desperately needs
creativity on display
for all of us to hear,
to see, to feel
in our bones.

Rebirth

The homeless near street corners
and in building alcoves
on sunny spring days,
their faces form these subtle smiles
as people with jobs and families
pass by with frowns.

The smiles display looks of triumph.
Men and women who've made it
through the brutal winds and famine
of winter, they've earned their moment
to bask under a renewed sun.

The few dollars collected
from the swarm of joggers
and students and dog walkers,
that's the small reward
for survival.

Unworthy Fight

A sparrow landed in a city park
near a fat black cat sprawled in the grass.
The bird began to chirp, chirp, chirp,
in the way drunkards ramble in bars.
Clearly irritated, the cat crouched low,
its ears back, ready to pounce.

After about a minute, the cat relaxed.
It must have figured killing the bird
would ruin the mellow mood of the day.
After all, there's no reason to kill for a meal
if someone is good enough to pour food
into a bowl every day.

A moment later, the bird took off
and vanished in the trees.
The cat flopped itself
back into the grass.

Flames to Independence

Sometimes a man needs
to stare at the flames
of a wood fire
and allow himself to be
transported from the flames
in his mind.

Other times, that man
must walk through the fires
of overseers and hucksters
that surround his days
and his nights.

Stepping onto the coals
may burn his shoes and socks.
The heat may singe his feet.
Still, if that man wants to survive,
he must walk forward, ever forward,
through the flames.

Wiped

One day I will die.
I'm reconciled to that truth.
My own death does not concern me.
What does twist my gut
is the black teenage boy who knocks on doors
in the suburban white neighborhood.
He looks for odd jobs and new friends.
That boy really digs pot and bicycles,
girls, video games, and basketball.
One day, an older resident, propagandized
by cable news and talk radio,
they will call the cops
in paralyzed fear,
and then that boy
will be wiped from the face
of the Earth.

GOING HOME TIME WHISTLE

Before the Storm

A middle-aged man at the bus stop
in checkered chef's pants
sat on the bench alone.
Bent over at the waist,
he held his head in his hands
after what appeared to be
a hard day on the job.

'How's life today?' I said.
'I'm just trying to stay alive,'
the chef said in a deep voice
that carried meaning, soul.

Dark clouds rolled toward us,
they quickly blocked out the summer light.
The chef stared aimlessly down the road.
I watched two young women
in booty shorts jiggle their behinds
through a crosswalk.

That chef and I occupied
the street corner in silent hope
that our bus would arrive
before the downpour.

Delusion

I had a dream
on the bus ride home
that money didn't matter.
We were too busy
caring about each other.
Shortly thereafter, I woke
and realized the truth.
We've allowed greed to win.

Snot Liberation

Sitting in traffic after the job,
a guy wearing a golf shirt in the car next to me
picked his nose hard and with passion.
After several seconds of labor,
the golf shirt pulled out a huge wad
of snot, his reward.
The grin on that man's face
revealed a true sense of triumph,
a sincere mark of joy
that he,
and he alone,
for a brief time,
had taken back control
of his life.

Illicit Relief

Bourbon after the job
always pours over the tongue
a little sweeter when it comes
from an illegal flask
while sitting by the river
in the city.
An old fisherman nearby
wearing a dirty cap,
he licks his lips
in envy.

Friday Dreams

We scratched lottery tickets
at the table on Friday nights.
After a hard week and still no money,
those tickets held our dreams of better days.
The tickets were usually losers,
but every once in a while
we'd hit for five bucks,
and the dreams would continue
through another week.

Laces

On the foot rail along the bar
there are many kinds of shoes
resting next to each other.
Black heels lean against muddy work boots.
Basketball and skateboard sneakers
kick the rail next to brown wingtips.

The shoes come from different places.
Each pair lives within a unique culture.
After a long week at jobs and universities,
the shoes take a well-earned rest
while their owners laugh and drink
as friends, together.

Guilt Scrub

No matter how many showers
I take in the evenings
or in the afternoons,
it's impossible to wash away
the pernicious scent
of deception.
We try and we try,
but only time and guilt
can do the job.
It's almost never possible
to know how long the foulness
will linger.

See Me Through

Opening one's soul to the public
is to swim naked in the sewer
with scores of salivating rats.
The poseurs spill their low-calorie
compliments. The haters,
they drop the most sincere insults.
Depressed, angry, mad,
I walked into the kitchen.
Standing barefoot on the cracked tiles,
Hemingway finally made sense.
A bottle of cheap whiskey
next to the coffee maker,
it had a mouthful left to go.
I figured it would see me through
and that's precisely
what it did.

Pretenders

Few people in bars these days
have dirty fingernails.
Disillusioned young men and women sit on stools
with hair products and designer threads
as they pretend substance.

Lies of false friendships,
the constant positioning for value,
the brand marketing of self,
it oozes from their pores in the form
of facial scrubs and beard oils.

In a quest for favor, power,
the pretenders have used purity
as a replacement for morality
to destroy workers with dirty fingernails
and imperfect philosophies.

In mass hordes of hairless bodies,
the disillusioned climb over each other
in a perfumed pit of their own design.
Without easy targets to take out,
they plot against and feast upon
their own kind, and anyone else
with the guts to speak truth.

Splatter

Distrust is not necessarily formed
from the telling of lies.
Lying plays its role
most days of our lives.
When the boss questions our late arrival,
we lie. When a lover weeps
in irrational jealousy,
we lie. The so-called flavor
we add to our stories
to build vain popularity
among co-workers and bar flies
and our women,
they're all acceptable
lies.

...however...

When we splatter the thick sludge
of betrayal across our invisible connections,
that's what pollutes the minds
of those we love
or hold dear.

Seeking Viewpoints

Everyone knows our perspectives
change when we climb
to high places.
Familiar surroundings
take on a fresh view
from fresh eyes.

The wise elders and the teachers,
they always allow us to independently
discover the dramatic differences
in our interpretations
based on where we stand.

The landscape we behold
from the orderly rungs
of an approved ladder
is never quite the same sight
as when we find a way to perch
atop a graffiti-strewn wall.

Take it Back

I often hear in the bars
that life isn't always fair
from the mouths of scorned lovers
and underpaid wage servants.

Fairness, I've learned, is usually emotional.
It's based on a sense of control.
The less power we have
over our own lives,
the less fair life feels.

Maybe that's why all these old nuns
and Buddhists and missionaries
walk between the raindrops,
grinning ear to ear.
They've found a sense of peace
that follows them all the way
to the grave.

Firefly

One summer evening,
after driving home from the job,
I encountered a firefly
that lay dying
between a couple of stones
in my gravel parking space.

The poor bug's light bulb
flickered and dimmed
with its final breaths.

Though the firefly owed no money
and was not forced into labor,
the creature found the courage
and the will to fulfill its purpose
for the benefit of others.

I stood in silent reverence
during the firefly's final minutes,
writing satchel over my shoulder.
The bug gave us the gifts
of light and beauty and hope.
It did this selfless work
until the last bit of its magic
faded into darkness.

Self-Portrait

Observing suburban culture
can diminish passion for life.
The poet looks upon sanitized people
that represent the last remnants
of the American experiment.

The poet yawns in apathy
and then streams some Mahler
through his earbuds
to shrug off the numbness.

Part of the poet's mind is conflicted
with the desire to spark change
and reverse the slow decline.
Another part of his mind
is bored with the view.

Take it Home

A sexy brunette nursed a beer
and chatted to a few people
inside a local bar.
She had a curvaceous figure,
not fat, just on the thicker side,
and she had these full lips
that captured every man's attention.
The dame wore this little black skirt
that showed off thick, muscular legs
littered with tiny cuts, bruises,
and patches of red skin.

I said hello and she politely smiled.
'What do you do?' she said.
'Writer. How about you?'
'I work in a warehouse.'
'Damn, that's hard work.'
'Yeah it is,' she said with pride,
'but at least I don't take it home with me.'
I didn't have the heart to tell her
that yeah, actually,
she really did.

Tastes of Pleasure

Whiskey and women,
the two most immersive vices
of delight and pain.
They both must be enjoyed regularly,
but in cautious moderation.
After a hard day, that first taste
goes down smooth,
as if the silky caress of heaven
crossed one's soot-covered lips.
Dive too deep, and those pleasures
will turn to the most violent
form of betrayal.

Salvation

Sitting on a picnic bench
next to the river, a dark torment
took control of my thoughts.
After years of anguish, I finally allowed
the steady rhythm of the river's current
to transport me from the physical world.
In that moment, a flood of past sins
rampaged through my mind.
A dull ache ran through my bones.

Just as the talons of madness began to claw
and shred my corrupt soul,
the river offered to absorb my sins.

Polluted as those memories were,
I chose to hold on to a few transgressions
that have defined my truth.
The others, I expelled into the water.
With the strength of a guardian angel
that has battled many bitter demons,
the river carried away my sins.
It then promised me the torment
would not return.

Soft Distraction

When life refuses to go
your way, and the madness
takes control, drink looks sexier
than that one dame at the bar.
You know her. She's the distraction
with the red lips and troubled eyes,
the one every drunkard in the joint
wants to press against.
She's the reminder
that our problems are trivial
when compared side by side
to her nightmare.

One Guy

This one guy in the bar,
his face drooped from a fatigue of life.
That kind of numbness,
it's worse than loneliness.
When you're lonely,
that means you're still trying.
When you've gone dull,
something or someone
convinced you
to give up.

So, this guy says to me,
"Why do you write?"
I say, "Because I have to."
He says, "I don't get it."
I agreed.

Look in the mirror

Every last one of us
has the capacity to love
our neighbors and support
communities in need.
Each of us also suffers
the intoxicating temptations
of wealth, self-righteous fury,
and violence.
To achieve wisdom,
we must first recognize
our sins.

Refuse to Hate

On the city sidewalk, a middle-aged woman
in dirty jeans and a torn flannel shirt
sat with her legs crossed.
Long, tangled brown hair obscured her face
as her head tilted forward
to read a paperback novel,
its front cover torn away.
A white cardboard sign leaned
against her knee that read,
'I REFUSE TO HATE.'

An attractive young couple walked by,
dressed in polished cowboy boots,
suburban country music attire.
They kept their eyes forward
and their mouths shut.
At the corner, a few yards away,
the couple waited to cross the street.
'They can read?' the young woman said.
Her date chuckled.

Back on the sidewalk,
the homeless woman coughed,
and then turned the page.

Refill

That bartender poured my bourbon
and took an interest in my life.
'What's wrong, pal?
You can tell me.
I have all the answers.'

‘That’s great,' I said,
'but I don't know
any of the questions.'

For the rest of the night,
he left me with my typer
and silently refilled
the bourbon.

Doldrums

The problem with people-watching
in the middling suburbs outside Pittsburgh,
is everyone looks like they're related,
a little too similar, bad photocopies
of the same dull morality.

The girls have similar haircuts
while the boys wear similar shorts.
The men and women,
they cannot stomach the 'F' word,
but they adore efficient order
enforced through totalitarian violence.

Chemical air fresheners are pumped
through department store ventilation systems.
Perhaps that chemical compound is designed
to induce complacency for the status quo
and suppress everyone's style
or sense of fashion.

Bullshit in Waiting

Sitting on a bench inside the mall,
I waited to have a watch repaired
at some old man's jewelry kiosk.
A young woman in a little black dress
carrying a large gold purse
strolled in front of me and stopped,
her gaze focused intently
on an oversized smartphone.

The woman's round ass and tanned thighs
would have made for a tight fuck,
but with far too many consequences.
Her perfect makeup and expensive shoes
indicated a bored, spoiled daughter
of professional parents,
a housewife in waiting.
One could almost smell her fertility
in the mall's manufactured air,
the repressive instincts to establish
a three bedroom suburban prison.

A small black tattoo, larger than a quarter,
adorned the woman's right foot.
The tattoo was two letter *'Cs'* back to back,
in the shape of the designer label
emblazoned on her gold purse.

I desperately needed a shot of scotch
as the maddening truth blurred
my vision under the bright mall lights.
For all the political rhetoric and activism

to confront violent racism or classism,
little energy is spent on our need
for creative, independent thought.

We are no longer freethinking individuals,
but rather the subjects of brand marketing.
Placed into cultural demographics,
the young and the old are instructed
on what to eat and what to believe.
Few people still resist such control,
and our numbers are shrinking.

Consumers

In the most ferocious winter storms,
there are people of honor
who will share their gloves.
During times of war,
some children continue to dream.
When famine strikes,
old men find the will
to be generous with their soup.
In a mall parking lot,
drivers will ram you to death
for a spot ten feet closer
to the door.

Falcon Poets

The image of barren tree branches,
black, lonely, forsaken,
set against the backdrop
of a blue sky and white clouds,
that's the perfect metaphor of life.
Some days we're the tree.
Other times, we're falcons
that soar through the air
as poets of destiny.

Remember and Forget

There are moments,
frozen capsules of time,
burned into our brains.
Those memories feel
as if they'll outlive us.
Then there are the moments
that are forever lost,
and when a lover or friend
tells the story years later,
we quietly mourn
that memory's death.

Rainy Ponderings

Rainy Sunday mornings
are the primary fuel
for the most thoughtful
ponderings,
daydreams,
prayers.

While the hovering quilt of dark clouds
suffocates many external ambitions
for personal achievement,
that tapestry in the sky
is ready to accept
the art that lives deep
within each of us.
All we must do
is release it.

Rest and Reading

Inside the bookstore café,
an overweight woman wedged herself
between the arms of a wooden chair.
Her black, greasy sneakers,
resembled long hours
on a diner's kitchen floor.

That woman then opened a hardcover novel
and rested the spine on her stomach.
Reading and sipping a coffee,
she wore a permanent smile.
Without much cash or clean shoes,
that badass taught us all
a valuable lesson
in happiness.

Acerbic Attitude

On the city bike trail,
an older man without shoes
or a shirt casually pedaled
a rickety red bicycle
while smoking a fat cigar.
The man’s smiling eyes
and sunburned shoulders
conveyed a level of carefree joy
most of us hope to achieve.
At least we now know
it's possible.

Paper-Thin

As the mind grows older,
fewer aspects of modern life and culture
make any kind of sense.
The previous generation constructs
narrow interpretations of the world,
a panicked, paper-thin box
to slow down human progress.

Resentment of age and change
leads our weakened fingers
to grip these cardboard boxes
of old items and stale ideas
we can still comprehend.
Fortunately for all of humanity,
no matter how tight our grip,
the boxes eventually collapse
and slip away.
Our ideas and notions
are forced to evolve.
The boxes are recycled
as the new generation
redefines the world
in their own image.

Crackle

There are few moments
more soothing than a warm evening
and the crackle of a fire.
In these hypnotic moments,
a young woman can dream
about her future.
Fathers with calloused palms
can sit in silence
with their thoughts and their sins.
The old, after a lifetime of struggle,
they can reflect upon the past
with an invaluable wisdom
the others do not realize
they have yet to possess.

Discovered Moral Truth

In a dream, Mark Twain
and I sat in lawn chairs
smoking cigars on a summer day.
He laughed about the greed
of men who use moral truth
to justify the acquisition
of wealth and power.

'If you want to find real morality,'
the scratchy-voiced author said,
'look to the radicals.'
'Why?' I asked.
'Isn't it obvious? The radicals
know how to love,
and that is the fuel
of all human progress.'

'What about instinct,' I said,
'the survival of the fittest?
Surely, survival is more important
than love?'

Twain squinted at me
as he rolled the cigar between his teeth.
'What a mean and hateful time
you live in,' he said. 'Survival
is for animals. The work of humans
in civilization is to live together
and thrive together.'

'I don't know,' I said. 'Radicals are always

on the fringe, never happy with the way things are.
How can anyone not grounded in the here and now
ever hold to a moral truth?'

The author pulled a righteous smile
across his face. 'All things, my boy,
have a beginning, a central starting point.
A train cannot travel if it does not depart a station.
The radicals are on a journey of progress.
The here and now, as you put it,
is the station they depart.
Love and compassion are the coals
that keeps them moving forward
to find new frontiers.'

I found it difficult to disagree,
and the cigar carried the smoky taste
of bourbon next to a campfire.

Old Friend

If reliability is the measurement
of friendship, my best amigo
is the late night madness
that never fails to visit.

While psychotics without consciences
and the martyrs with limited vision
sleep like the dead,
my old friend arrives.
He whispers musings
to me
about countless old sins.
He reminds me
my days are numbered.

Late Night Thoughts

In the quiet of night,
the demons murmur
just under the surface.
Too tired to sleep,
worries replace rational thoughts.
There are no more distractions
to hide our truths.
We have no choice
but to swim in the toxic
pool of our sins.

Thank you, dear hater

In the great bounty of sinners
from which you could choose,
please know how touched I am
that you've selected me
as the target of your revulsion.
The more your stomach churns
at my words and my presence,
that rage provides me
the necessary fuel
for my work.

As the cruel march of time goes on,
our spirits will eventually unwind
and this vicious chapter will close.
To be honest, I hope I go first.
I couldn't stomach the idea
that I've denied you the satisfaction
to outlive an enemy.

That simple wish is the least I can do
for the one who has provided me
the energy to build a legacy
that will outlive me
and outlast you.

Behind Walls

Solitude is an elixir.
Alone has been my predilection
since first entering the workforce
and the boss found a way to sexualize
the gratifying pleasures of malice.
While others may drown
in a great lake of loneliness,
solitude and a shot of whiskey,
to some of us, can make
for a lovely escape.

Shooing the Demons

Sometimes writing words,
that great battle of the soul,
fights off late night demons.
Other times, masturbation
to free porn does the trick.
A quiet prayer and meditation
almost always eases the mind.
When all else fails,
a trusty glass of bourbon
floats the imagination
into dreams.

Back to Reality

After a passionate night,
she asked me to drop her off
at the job. I pulled up to the curb
and watched her step out
into the drizzle.
I gazed at her hips
as she strolled to the door,
but the car behind me blew its horn.
The reality brought me back to Earth.
Our date had ended.

Contented

Drunk on the orange light of dusk.
High on drink in a thick glass.
Cocooned in cigar smoke that hovers,
it carries the scent of a sweet menace.
The best part is knowing your balls hang
out of sweaty boxers on the back stoop
while the neighbor lady stares
out the window, ashamed
of the visual rape,
the total disdain
of her orderly life.

It's then you realize, that's it baby.
The concert of life has reached its crescendo.
A spontaneous smile begins to form,
as you also begin to understand,
these small pleasures are
all you ever wanted
in the first place.

Turn the page for an important message from our benevolent corporate board of directors.

Rant of a Spiraling Society

As a writer who absorbs the world and then bleeds his truth, I'm finding it harder and harder to reach new readers. I feel as if I'm forced to break through brick walls of political propaganda that television, radio, and web media have conjured to dominate and control so many minds in the United States and other English-speaking regions. I've watched the public relations and marketing industries relentlessly pursue keywords and phrases to provoke the irrational parts of our brains. The goal of these actions is to persuade emotional investment in products and services, pollution and politicians. So much noxious programming, I fear, has cut off our ability to form independent thoughts and true relationships.

I can work around this programming in small ways by steering clear of keywords and by introducing abstract moral truths. The moment I reference terms such as *equality*, *democracy*, or *justice*, my work is often met with fervent rage from social media users. Worse yet, there are times my words don't even scrape the hardened crust of these propagandized souls. The work then goes completely ignored as people allow their minds to gravitate toward hate speech.

I feel myself losing touch with a society that I've taken for granted my entire writing life. In a gluttonous feast of sensational media that has proven nearly impossible to extricate ourselves, we allow the power of profiteers and con-artists to stream content into our minds. That messaging programs us to accept unprecedented levels of violence and resentment for others across the cultural divide. For the past 10 years or more, I've seen and heard a growing number people cheer for the heartache of others.

In a hateful orgy of resentment, a large swath of society has proven comfortable with exterminating or incarcerating human beings for the color of their skin, religious doctrines, or the origin of their birth in private for-profit prisons. We've grown comfortable with selling off our imperfect bodies to greedy insurance companies that scheme and plot against humanity to increase revenues. Few of us take moral stands against domestic violence.

Morality is weakness.
The ecosystem we rely on for life is fake.
Love is a mental disorder.
Children are targets of projectile weapons.
More cops. More guns. More enemies.

Yes, I definitely feel we are lost in a spiral of human descent, where there is no end, only a continuous state of torment and misery and despair.

End rant.

Of course, there are plenty of happy moments in our lives that are woven into the bleak portrait I just illustrated. There's beauty in the good works of so many people around us. The situations in my rant, however, are quite real, and that poison is spreading. It will never be cured by ignoring it. We must find a way to fortify our souls to withstand the toxic lies and violent actions that so often crash down upon us. That's achieved by tearing ourselves away from talking heads, and instead we must expend the energy to learn our truths. We must then help others discover their truths for the benefit of society.

Truth has always been and will always be the tonic for poisoned minds.

—Ron Gavalik

About the Author

Ron Gavalik is a writer
in Pittsburgh, Pennsylvania.
You can stalk him online.
He likes whiskey.

www.ingramcontent.com/pod-product-compliance
Lightning Source LLC
LaVergne TN
LVHW051412080426
835508LV00022B/3047

* 9 7 8 1 7 3 2 0 6 9 7 4 9 *